Four American Folk Hymns

1. SAINTS BOUND FOR HEAVEN

A Melody from Walker's
Southern Harmony, 1835

Arranged by Mack Wilberg

OXFORD
UNIVERSITY PRESS

SAINTS BOUND FOR HEAVEN

(No. 1 from *Four American Folk Hymns)*

for SATB Choir and Piano Four-Hands

Melody from Walker's *Southern Harmony*, 1835
Arranged by MACK WILBERG

SOP., ALTO

TEN., BASS

Our ___ bond-age it shall end ___ by and by, by and by, our ___ bond-age it shall

end___ by and by. From___ E-gypt's yoke__ set free, hail the glo-rious ju - bi -

lee, and to Ca - naan we'll re - turn___ by and by, by and by, and to

Then with all the hap-py throng_ we'll re-joice, we'll re-joice, then with all the hap-py

throng_ we'll re-joice. Shout-ing glo-ry to_ our King, till the vaults of heav-en

joice,   we'll re - joice!_____